W9-BAQ-802

ANIMAL FEATHERS & FUR

David M. Schwartz *is an award-winning author of children's books, on a wide variety of topics, loved by children around the world.* Dwight Kuhn's *scientific expertise and artful eye work together with the camera to capture the awesome wonder of the natural world.*

For a free color catalog describing Gareth Stevens Publishing's list of high-quality books and multimedia programs, call 1-800-542-2595 (USA) or 1-800-461-9120 (Canada). Gareth Stevens Publishing's Fax: (414) 225-0377.

Library of Congress Cataloging-in-Publication Data

Schwartz, David M.
    Animal feathers & fur / by David M. Schwartz; photographs by Dwight Kuhn.
      p. cm. — (Look once, look again)
    Includes bibliographical references (p. 23) and index.
    Summary: Introduces, in simple text and photographs, the feathers or fur of a
yellow warbler, porcupine, skunk, white-tailed deer, flying squirrel, owl, and dalmatian.
    ISBN 0-8368-2424-5 (lib. bdg.)
    1. Fur—Juvenile literature. 2. Feathers—Juvenile literature. [1. Fur. 2. Feathers.
3. Animals—Habits and behavior.] I. Kuhn, Dwight, ill. II. Title. III. Series: Schwartz,
David M. Look once, look again.
QL942.S35 1999
573.5'8—dc21   99-18611

This North American edition first published in 1999 by
Gareth Stevens Publishing
1555 North RiverCenter Drive, Suite 201
Milwaukee, Wisconsin 53212 USA

First published in the United States in 1998 by Creative Teaching Press, Inc., P.O. Box 6017, Cypress, California, 90630-0017.

Text © 1998 by David M. Schwartz; photographs © 1998 by Dwight Kuhn. Additional end matter © 1999 by Gareth Stevens, Inc.

Printed in the United States of America

1 2 3 4 5 6 7 8 9 03 02 01 00 99

ANIMAL FEATHERS & FUR

by David M. Schwartz

photographs by Dwight Kuhn

A SPRINGBOARDS INTO SCIENCE SERIES

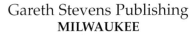

Gareth Stevens Publishing

MILWAUKEE

A tail like this is for the ...

...birds. The stiff feathers on a bird's tail help it steer through the air. When it wants to turn quickly, a bird tips its tail feathers sideways. This bird is called a yellow warbler.

This animal's fur
is spiny, not furry.
You wouldn't want
to pet it!

The "hairs" of a porcupine are long and sharp. They are called quills. When a porcupine senses danger, it raises its quills. If a predator tries to bite a porcupine, it gets a mouthful of quills.

A porcupine's quills can come out of its skin, but a porcupine cannot shoot its quills.

8

The black-and-white fur of this animal says,
"Watch out — or else!"

Phew! Nothing else smells like a skunk — or looks like one. Its black-and-white fur helps protect the skunk. Other animals remember it and run the other way!

Whose tail is brown on one
side and white on the other?

11

When a white-tailed deer's tail is down, the white fur does not show. When the deer senses danger, it raises its tail like a white flag. The white fur tells other deer that danger is near. Off they run!

This animal spreads its legs wide to become a flying carpet!

13

A flying squirrel can't really fly. When it wants to leap to another tree, the squirrel spreads its legs to stretch the loose skin on the sides of its body. The skin acts like a cape. It allows the squirrel to glide through the air. As a flying squirrel glides, it steers with its tail.

These soft, frilly feathers belong to a hunter of the night.

15

An owl must fly silently through the woods at night. It does not want to be heard while it hunts. Owl feathers are soft. They are fringed at the edge. Soft, fringed feathers make little noise. The owl wants to surprise its prey.

In a famous story, 101 animals had spots like these.

Dalmatians are famous for their spots, but the puppies are born pure white. They get their spots when they are about three or four weeks old.

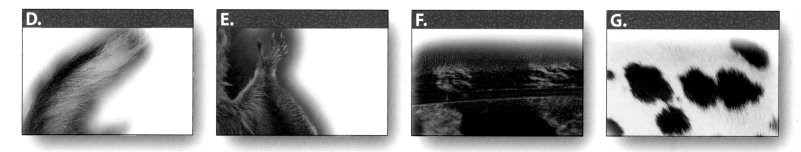

Look closely. Can you name these animals?

A. Yellow warbler

B. Porcupine

C. Skunk

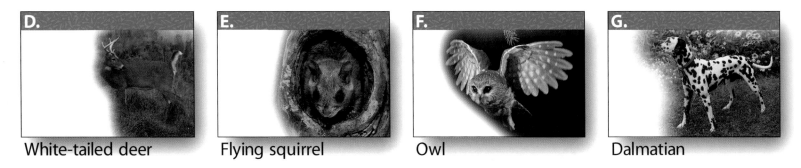

D. White-tailed deer

E. Flying squirrel

F. Owl

G. Dalmatian

How many were you able to identify correctly?

cape: an outer garment or item of clothing that does not have sleeves. It hangs loosely over the shoulders.

dalmatian: a large dog that has a short, white coat with black or brown spots.

frilly: having a fringe or other similar, delicate decoration.

fringed: edged with hanging threads or strips. The edges of some bedspreads and scarves are decorated in this way.

glides: moves in a smooth and easy way.

predator: an animal that hunts other animals for food.

prey: an animal that is hunted by other animals for food.

quills: the sharp, hollow spines on the body of a porcupine.

senses (v): becomes aware of something, or knows about it, through any of the five senses — hearing, seeing, smelling, tasting, and touching.

silently: done without making any sound.

spiny: covered with sharp and pointed spines that stick out from the body, like the quills of a porcupine.

steer: to direct the course of something.

stiff: not easily bent, like a thick piece of cardboard.

warbler: a small type of songbird that eats mainly insects.

ACTIVITIES

Owl Adaptations

An adaptation develops slowly over time to help an animal or plant survive. For example, an owl has fringed feathers that help it silently reach its prey. Find the picture of the owl in this book, and look at it carefully. Then make a list of other adaptations that help the owl as a hunter.

Spots and Stripes

Play a "spots and stripes" guessing game. Think of an animal that has either spots or stripes (you could look in books about animals to get some ideas). Then have friends or family members ask you "yes" or "no" questions to try to guess what animal you are thinking of. For example, they might ask, "Do you have spots?" Next, they might ask, "Do you live in the woods?" See if they can guess the animal you are thinking of in ten questions or less.

Hair's Looking at You!

Visit a pet store to see and compare the different kinds of hair or fur that dogs, cats, and other pets have. Find the animal with the longest hair and with the softest fur. Do you see coats that are spotted or striped?

Hello, Yellow!

In a bird book, find a picture of a yellow warbler. Look through the book for other kinds of yellow birds, such as a goldfinch. How are the feathers of the other birds different from the yellow warbler? How are they alike?

Fantastic Feathers

Find an article in an encyclopedia that labels the parts of a feather. On a real feather, can you see the quill, the shaft, the barbs, and the barbules (the little hooks that hold the feather together)?

More Books to Read

Birds. Young Scientist Concepts & Projects (series). Jen Green (Gareth Stevens)

Birds. Wonderful World of Animals (series). Beatrice MacLeod (Gareth Stevens)

The Dalmatian. Charlotte Wilcox (Capstone Press)

Flying Animals. Wings (series). Patricia Lantier-Sampon (Gareth Stevens)

Flying Squirrels. Lynn M. Stone (Rourke)

The Porcupine. Victoria Sherrow (Silver Burdett)

Skunks. Lynn M. Stone (Rourke)

Videos

Birds. (United Learning)

Dalmatians at Play. (Matrix Media)

On Silent Wings. (Beacon Films)

Web Sites

members.aol.com/owlbox/owlhome.htm

www.akc.org/

Some web sites stay current longer than others. For further web sites, use your search engines to locate the following topics: *birds, dalmatians, deer, dogs, feathers, porcupines,* and *skunks.*

INDEX